A Little Bit
of God's Wisdom & Wit
for Men

Written and Compiled by
Clift Richards & Lloyd Hildebrand

Victory House, Inc.
Tulsa, Oklahoma

A LITTLE BIT OF GOD'S WISDOM AND WIT FOR MEN
Copyright © 1994 by K & C International, Inc.
ISBN: 0-932081-43-6
Printed in the United States of America

Published by Victory House, Inc.
P.O. Box 700238
Tulsa, Oklahoma 74170
(918) 747-5009

Cover Design by : *Whitley Graphics*

INTRODUCTION

As G.K. Chesterton wrote, "Wit is a sword; it is meant to make people feel the point as well as see it." We trust that you will feel the wisdom presented in this handy book and that you will see it as well. Small enough to be taken anywhere, men designed this book for men; its quotations and quips relate to the concerns and issues faced by men in our fast-paced society.

A veritable smorgasbord of food for thought and reflection, *A Little Bit of God's Wisdom and Wit for Men* presents truths that you can take hold of, comic-relief from your daily tensions, inspiration to brighten your day and wisdom to apply to your life. Its glistening gems of humor and honesty will challenge you lead you into new dimensions of personal growth.

Common-sense sayings of great men like Oswald Chambers, Ben Franklin, C.S. Lewis, Mark Twain, George Muller, Omar Bradley and others will open windows to fresh insights for your mind and spirit as you learn from the experiences of others in surprising ways.

To Our Readers

If you have favorite humorous or wise sayings or anecdotes that we could include in future books, please send them to:

Clift Richards & Lloyd Hildebrand
c/o Victory House, Inc.
P.O. Box 700238
Tulsa, OK 74170

Other Books of Interest

A Little Bit of God's Wisdom and Wit
A Little Bit of God's Wisdom and Wit for Men
A Little Bit of God's Wisdom and Wit for Women
Prayers That Prevail — The Believer's Manual of Prayers
Prayers That Prevail for America — Changing a Nation Through Prayer
Prayers That Prevail for Your Children — A Parent's and Grandparent's
   Manual of Prayers

All titles are available at your local
bookstore or through Victory House, Inc.

Bravery is the capacity to perform properly even when scared half to death.

(General Omar N. Bradley)

———◆•◆———

The Lord is my light and my salvation; whom shall I fear? the Lord is the strength of my life; of whom shall I be afraid?
(Psalm 27:1).

Even if you are on the right track, you'll get run over if you just sit there.

(Will Rogers)

No matter what your vocation, you are called to serve others.

---◆·◆---

For all the law is fulfilled in one word, even in this; Thou shalt love thy neighbour as thyself (Galatians 5:14).

A man involved in a shady business never has a sunny life.

❖——◆●◆——❖

Now I pray to God that ye do no evil;...that ye should do that which is honest (2 Corinthians 13:7).

Faith is to believe what you do not yet see; the reward for this faith is to see what you believe.

(St. Augustine)

Now faith is the substance of things hoped for, the evidence of things not seen (Hebrews 11:1).

An honest man's the noblest work of God.

(Alexander Pope)

Keep thee far from a false matter (Exodus 23:7).

Keep thy eyes wide open before marriage, and half shut afterwards.

(Benjamin Franklin)

And they shall be one flesh (Genesis 2:24).

Money is a good servant but a bad master.

(H.G. Bohn)

————◆•◆————

Ye cannot serve God and mammon (Matthew 6:24).

The great secret of morals is love.

(Percy Bysshe Shelley)

❖•❖

Above all these things put on charity, which is the bond of perfectness (Colossians 3:14).

You cannot be a true man until you learn to obey.

(Robert E. Lee)

—◆•◆—

Walk in all his ways (Joshua 22:5).

The proud hate pride —
in others.

(Benjamin Franklin)

———◆•◆———

How are the mighty fallen (2 Samuel 1:19).

These three things deplete man's strength: fear, travel, and sin.

(Hebrew proverb)

◆•◆

In quietness and in confidence shall be your strength (Isaiah 30:15).

Do not trust the man that tells you all his troubles but keeps from you his joys.

(Hebrew proverb)

Blessed is the man that maketh the Lord his trust (Psalm 40:4).

No wise man ever wished to be younger.

(Jonathan Swift)

The glory of young men is their strength: and the beauty of old men is the gray head (Proverbs 20:29).

For success knock the t off of can't.

---◆•◆---

*I can do everything through him who gives me strength
(Philippians 4:13, NIV).*

Prayer changes the attitudes of your heart.

❖

By prayer and supplication with thanksgiving let your requests be made known unto God (Philippians 4:6).

Are your priorities in order?

But seek ye first the kingdom of God, and his righteousness; and all these things shall be added unto you (Matthew 6:33).

Making marriage work is like running a farm. You have to start all over again each morning.

(The Way of St. Francis)

❖

Nevertheless let every one of you in particular so love his wife even as himself; and the wife see that she reverence her husband (Ephesians 5:33).

The world has yet to see what God can do when a man is totally surrendered to Him. By God's grace, I intend to be that man.

(Dwight L. Moody)

Commit thy works unto the Lord, and thy thoughts shall be established (Proverbs 16:3).

What matters is not the size of the dog in a fight, but the size of the fight in the dog.

You are of God, little children, and have overcome them, because He who is in you is greater than he who is in the world (1 John 4:4, NKJV).

Most people are about as happy as they make up their minds to be.

❖•❖

Why are you downcast, O my soul? Why so disturbed within me? Put your hope in God, for I will yet praise him, my Savior and my God (Psalm 43:5).

Always do right. This will gratify some people and astonish the rest.

(Mark Twain)

A mighty oak started life as a little acorn.

And he shall be like a tree planted by the rivers of water, that bringeth forth his fruit in his season; his leaf also shall not wither; and whatsoever he doeth shall prosper (Psalm 1:3).

Babe Ruth long held the record for the most strike-outs as well as the most home runs.

◆•◆

Let us not be weary in well doing: for in due season we shall reap, if we faint not (Galatians 6:9).

You can dislocate your shoulder when you pat yourself on the back.

———◆•◆———

Shall the axe boast itself against him that heweth therewith? or shall the saw magnify itself against him that shaketh it? (Isaiah 10:15).

To belittle is to be little; to be grateful is to be great.

But David encouraged himself in the Lord his God (1 Samuel 30:6).

The person who kneels often knows how to stand fast.

The effectual fervent prayer of a righteous man availeth much (James 5:16).

God's Word is a hammer that constructs a life.

Is not my word like as a fire? saith the Lord; and like a hammer that breaketh the rock in pieces? (Jeremiah 23:29).

Blessed are they who mind their own business.

But let none of you suffer as a...busybody in other men's matters (1 Peter 4:15).

Be sure and praise your wife, even if it shocks her.

Plan ahead. Noah didn't wait until the rain came to start the ark.

By faith Noah, being warned of God of things not seen as yet, moved with fear, prepared an ark to the saving of his house (Hebrews 11:7).

How do others see you?

◆•◆

Wherefore by their fruits ye shall know them (Matthew 7:20).

God's alarm clock has no snooze button.

———◆•◆———

He that keepeth thee will not slumber (Psalm 121:3).

The man who thinks he has no faults has at least one.

Pride goeth before destruction, and an haughty spirit before a fall (Proverbs 16:18).

Lazy people have many plans — for tomorrow.

❖•❖

As a door turns on its hinges, So does the lazy man on his bed (Proverbs 26:14, NKJV).

Success is a matter of your backbone, not your wishbone.

Commit thy works unto the Lord, and thy thoughts shall be established (Proverbs 16:3).

Some people who are waiting for their ship to come in have never sent one out.

Be not deceived; God is not mocked: for whatsoever a man soweth, that shall he also reap (Galatians 6:7).

It's better to be a has-been than a never-was.

For the Lord himself shall descend from heaven with a shout, with the voice of the archangel, and with the trump of God: and the dead in Christ shall rise first (1 Thessalonians 4:16).

Let the wife make the husband glad to come home, and let him make her sorry to see him leave.

(Martin Luther)

Do all the good you can,
By all the means you can,
In all the ways you can,
In all the places you can,
At all the times you can,
To all the people you can,
As long as you ever can.

(John Wesley)

His mouth works quicker than his brain — he says things he hasn't even thought of yet.

Out of the abundance of the heart the mouth speaketh (Matthew 12:34).

Why worry? Worry is like a rocking chair, it will give you something to do but it won't get you anywhere.

———◆•◆———

Let not your heart be troubled, neither let it be afraid (John 14:27).

There are no great men, only great challenges that ordinary men are forced by circumstances to meet.

(Admiral William F. Halsey)

Be of good courage, and He shall strengthen your heart, all ye that hope in the Lord (Psalm 31:24).

A diamond is a chunk of coal that stayed on the job under pressure.

❖

Therefore, since we are surrounded by such a great cloud of witnesses, let us throw off everything that hinders and the sin that so easily entangles, and let us run with perseverance the race marked out for us (Hebrews 12:1, NIV).

A committee meeting is often a meeting of the bored.

❖

The will of the Lord be done (Acts 21:14).

Courage is almost a contradiction in terms. It means a strong desire to live, taking the form of a readiness to die.

(G.K. Chesterton)

———◆•◆———

Be of good courage (1 Chronicles 19:13).

Make at least one person happy each day — even if it's yourself!

Rejoice, and be exceeding glad (Matthew 5:12).

A man who is truly great never loses the heart of a child.

Whosoever shall not receive the kingdom of God as a little child, he shall not enter therein (Mark 10:15).

A rumor is about as hard to unspread as butter.

(Changing Times)

Mischief shall come upon mischief, and rumour shall be upon rumour (Ezekiel 7:26).

God gives us the changing seasons to teach us gratitude.

Continue in prayer, and watch in the same with thanksgiving (Colossians 4:2).

A man should be like tea, his real strength showing when he gets in hot water.

(The Irish Digest)

Blessed is the man that endureth temptation (James 1:12).

The easiest way to resist temptation is publicly.

(Franklin P. Jones)

◆—◆—◆

Confess your faults one to another, and pray one for another, that ye may be healed. The effectual fervent prayer of a righteous man availeth much (James 5:16).

Some folks treat God like a lawyer — they only go to Him when they're in trouble.

Call unto me, and I will answer thee, and shew thee great and mighty things, which thou knowest not (Jeremiah 33:3).

Look for a person's motives before you judge his actions.

---◆•◆---

Bear ye one another's burdens, and so fulfill the law of Christ (Galatians 6:2).

God's eye is on the sparrow, and He watches over you.

———◆•◆———

Do not fear therefore; you are of more value than many sparrows (Matthew 10:31, NKJV).

Happiness comes from within.

◆•◆

The kingdom of God is within you (Luke 17:21).

Talking the talk is easier than walking the walk.

—◆•◆—

And this is love, that we walk after his commandments (2 John 6).

Faith is a refusal to panic.

(D. Martyn Lloyd-Jones)

Let us hold fast the profession of our faith without wavering (Hebrews 10:23).

Faith is not shelter against difficulties, but belief in the face of all contradictions.

(Paul Tournier)

For we walk by faith, not by sight (2 Corinthians 5:7, NKJV).

The tragedy of life is not that it ends so soon, but that we wait so long to begin it.

(W.M. Lewis)

In Him was life; and the life was the light of men (John 1:4).

The power of prayer is immeasurable.

---◆•◆---

*The same Lord over all is rich unto all that call upon Him
(Romans 10:12).*

What's most important to you?

---◆•◆---

That in all things he might have the preeminence (Colossians 1:18).

It is a funny thing about life; if you refuse to accept anything but the best, you very often get it.

(W. Somerset Maugham)

Let us then approach the thone of grace with confidence, so that we may receive mercy and find grace to help us in our time of need (Hebrews 4:16, NIV).

There will be no need for "last resorts" if prayer is your first resort.

———◆•◆———

Men ought always to pray (Luke 18:1).

Ten years from today, what will you wish you had done now?

---◆•◆---

Behold, now is the accepted time (2 Corinthians 6:2).

Many a man expects his wife to be perfect and to understand why he isn't.

———◆•◆———

Husbands, love your wives, and be not bitter against them
(Colossians 3:19).

There is no more lovely relationship than a good marriage.

(Martin Luther)

I don't know who my grandfather was; I am much more concerned to know what his grandson will be.

(Abraham Lincoln)

❖

O God, thou hast taught me from my youth; and hitherto have I declared thy wondrous works (Psalm 71:17).

We owe to Scripture the same reverence which we owe to God.

(John Calvin)

Your word, O Lord, is eternal; it stands firm in the heavens (Psalm 119:89, NIV).

Most of us hate to see a poor loser — or a rich winner.

(Harold Coffin)

———◆•◆———

Thou shalt not covet (Exodus 20:17).

God is working His purposes out.

---◆•◆---

And we know that all things work together for good to them that love God, to them who are the called according to his purpose (Romans 8:28).

Faults are thick where love is thin.

(Danish proverb)

———◆•◆———

Charity shall cover the multitude of sins (1 Peter 4:8).

Our incomes are like shoes: if too small, they pinch: if too large we stumble.

(Colton)

◆•◆

And my God will meet all your needs according to his glorious riches in Christ Jesus (Philippians 4:19, NIV).

Pray without ceasing.

————◆•◆————

Rejoice evermore. Pray without ceasing. In every thing give thanks: for this is the will of God in Christ Jesus concerning you (1 Thessalonians 5:16–18).

Faith brings us to God, hope anchors us to God, and love makes us like God.

And now abide faith, hope, love, these three; but the greatest of these is love (1 Corinthians 13:13, NKJV).

The Bible is a living book because it is the Book of the living God.

◆•◆

For the word of God is living and active. Sharper than any double-edged sword, it penetrates even to dividing soul and spirit, joints and marrow; it judges the thoughts and attitudes of the heart (Hebrews 4:12, NIV).

Show courtesy to others not because they are necessarily gentlemen, but simply because you are.

Give none offence (1 Corinthians 10:32).

Where there's marriage without love, there will be love without marriage.

(Benjamin Franklin)

❖ • ❖

Husbands, love your wives, even as Christ also loved the church, and gave himself for it (Ephesians 5:25).

The Lord gets His best soldiers out of the highlands of affliction.

(Charles Haddon Spurgeon)

❖

I have chosen thee in the furnace of affliction (Isaiah 48:10).

When your job is tough, get tougher than the job.

Finally, my brethren, be strong in the Lord, and in the power of His might (Ephesians 6:10).

When you tell a secret, it may go in one ear and then in another, and then in another....

A talebearer revealeth secrets (Proverbs 11:13).

Impatience is waiting in a hurry.

❖ ◆ ❖

For ye have need of patience, that, after ye have done the will of God, ye might receive the promise (Hebrews 10:36).

Marriage is an investment that pays you dividends if you pay interest.

(Anonymous)

Submitting yourselves one to another in the fear of God
(Ephesians 5:21).

Be kind! Every person you meet is fighting a difficult battle.

And be ye kind one to another, tenderhearted, forgiving one another, even as God for Christ's sake hath forgiven you (Ephesians 4:32).

Jesus is the way.

Jesus saith unto him, I am the way, the truth, and the life: no man cometh unto the Father, but by me (John 14:6).

God's requirements are met by God's enablings.

---◆•◆---

Jesus said unto him, If thou canst believe, all things are possible to him that believeth (Mark 9:23).

Treasures in heaven are laid up only as treasures on earth are laid down.

---◆•◆---

But lay up for yourselves treasures in heaven, where neither moth nor rust doth corrupt, and where thieves do not break through nor steal: For where your treasure is, there will your heart be also (Matthew 6:20–21).

Christ's limitless resources meet our endless needs.

I can do all things through Christ which strengtheneth me (Philippians 4:13).

Too many people quit looking for work when they find a job.

(Hillsboro, IL Rotarian)

And beside this, giving all diligence, add to your faith virtue; and to virtue knowledge (2 Peter 1:5).

God looks for men who trust Him fully; in them He will show His power.

(Andrew Murray)

Trust in the Lord with all thine heart; and lean not unto thine own understanding. In all thy ways acknowledge him, and he shall direct thy paths (Proverbs 3:5-6).

Don't question your wife's judgment — look whom she married.

(Denver Post)

—◆•◆—

Husbands, love your wives, even as Christ also loved the church, and gave himself for it (Ephesians 5:25).

The greatest sum in addition is to count your blessings.

It is of the Lord's mercies that we are not consumed, because his compassions fail not (Lamentations 3:22).

Little is much if God is in it.

———◆•◆———

But Jesus beheld them, and said unto them, With men this is impossible; but with God all things are possible (Matthew 19:26).

God develops spiritual power in our lives through pressure of hard places.

(A.B. Simpson)

For we which live are alway delivered unto death for Jesus' sake, that the life also of Jesus might be made manifest in our mortal flesh (2 Corinthians 4:11).

It is not well for a man to pray cream and live skim milk.

(Henry Ward Beecher)

The thief cometh not, but for to steal, and to kill, and to destroy: I am come that they might have life, and that they might have it more abundantly (John 10:10).

Begin to know Him now, and finish never.

(Oswald Chambers)

◆•◆

Be still, and know that I am God: I will be exalted among the heathen, I will be exalted in the earth (Psalm 46:10).

There are no miracles to men who do not believe in them.

———◆•◆———

We walk by faith, not by sight (2 Corinthians 5:7).

The beginning of anxiety is the end of faith, and the beginning of true faith is the end of anxiety.

(George Muller)

❖

The just shall live by faith (Romans 1:17).

Fear knocked at the door.
Faith answered.
No one was there.

(Inscription at Hind's Head Inn in England)

—◆•◆—

Be not afraid, only believe (Mark 5:36).

You can become your strongest in your weakest moment.

———◆•◆———

But he said to me, "My grace is sufficient for you, for my power is made perfect in weakness." Therefore I will boast all the more gladly about my weaknesses, so that Christ's power may rest on me (2 Corinthians 12:9, NIV).

Don't put your thumb on the scale when you are weighing the faults of another person.

---◆•◆---

With what measure ye mete, it shall be measured to you again (Matthew 7:2).

The man who removes a mountain begins by carrying away small stones.

(Ancient Proverb)

Reflect upon your present blessings, of which every man has many; not on your past misfortunes, of which all men have some.

(Charles Dickens)

Bless the Lord, O my soul: and all that is within me, bless his holy name (Psalm 103:1).

It is more blessed to give than to receive.

Give, and it shall be given unto you; good measure, pressed down, and shaken together, and running over, shall men give into your bosom. For with the same measure that ye mete withal it shall be measured to you again (Luke 6:38).

You are never alone.

Lo, I am with you alway, even unto the end of the world. Amen (Matthew 28:20).

Study the Bible daily.

❖

These were more noble than those in Thessalonica, in that they received the word with all readiness of mind, and searched the scriptures daily, whether those things were so (Acts 17:11).

Nothing can happen that you and God can't handle together.

---◆•◆---

What shall we then say to these things? If God be for us, who can be against us? (Romans 8:31).

Life is tons of discipline.

(Robert Frost)

———◆•◆———

He who heeds discipline shows the way to life, but whoever ignores correction leads others astray (Proverbs 10:17, NIV).

First things first.

Wisdom is the principal thing; therefore get wisdom: and with all thy getting get understanding (Proverbs 4:7).

God is waiting for you here at this very moment.

(Michael Quoist)

———◆•◆———

In returning and rest shall ye be saved; in quietness and in confidence shall be your strength (Isaiah 30:15).

We need to forgive our brother seventy times seven not only for 490 offences but for one offence.

(C.S. Lewis)

Be ye angry, and sin not: let not the sun go down upon your wrath: And be ye kind one to another, tenderhearted, forgiving one another, even as God for Christ's sake hath forgiven you (Ephesians 4:26,32).

Man is the only animal that blushes — or needs to.

(Mark Twain)

———◆●◆———

My confusion is continually before me, and the shame of my face hath covered me (Psalm 44:15).

Let go, and let God.

◆◆

Now unto him that is able to do exceeding abundantly above all that we ask or think, according to the power that worketh in us, Unto him be glory in the church by Christ Jesus throughout all ages, world without end. Amen (Ephesians 3:20-21).

Obedience means marching right on whether we feel like it or not.

(Dwight L. Moody)

Behold, I set before you this day a blessing and a curse; A blessing, if ye obey the commandments of the Lord your God, which I command you this day: And a curse, if ye will not obey the commandments of the Lord your God (Deuteronomy 11:26–28).

It is easier to build a boy than to mend a man.

◆—◆•◆—◆

Train up a child in the way he should go: and when he is old, he will not depart from it (Proverbs 22:6).

God's Word will keep you from sin, but sin will keep you from God's Word.

———◆•◆———

Wherewithal shall a young man cleanse his way? by taking heed thereto according to thy word (Psalm 119:9).

A happy marriage is a long conversation that always seems too short.

(Andre Maurois)

For this cause shall a man leave his father and mother, and shall be joined unto his wife, and they two shall be one flesh (Ephesians 5:31).

The heaviest end of the cross lies ever on His shoulders. If He bids us carry a burden, He carries it also.

(Charles Haddon Spurgeon)

———◆●◆———

Come unto me, all ye that labour and are heavy laden, and I will give you rest. Take my yoke upon you, and learn of me; for I am meek and lowly in heart: and ye shall find rest unto your souls. For my yoke is easy, and my burden is light (Matthew 11:28-30).

Praise keeps what prayer has changed.

❖•❖

Thou art my God, and I will praise thee: thou art my God, I will exalt thee (Psalm 118:28).

A man wrapped up in himself makes a small parcel.

❖

But we have this treasure in earthen vessels, that the excellency of the power may be of God, and not of us (2 Corinthians 4:7).

Nothing is so strong as gentleness; nothing is so gentle as real strength.

(St. Francis de Sales)

———◆•◆———

Blessed are the meek: for they shall inherit the earth (Matthew 5:5).

More men fail through lack of purpose than through lack of talent.

(Billy Sunday)

Where there is no vision, the people perish: but he that keepeth the law, happy is he (Proverbs 29:18).

Count your blessings.

———◆•◆———

Enter into his gates with thanksgiving, and into his courts with praise: be thankful unto him, and bless his name (Psalm 100:4).

The world begins next door.

—◆●◆—

Thou shalt love thy neighbour (Matthew 5:43).

He that falls in love with himself will find no rival.

(Benjamin Franklin)

And he said to them all, If any man will come after me, let him deny himself, and take up his cross daily, and follow me (Luke 9:23).

Patience seems bitter, but its fruit is sweet.

But let patience have her perfect work, that ye may be perfect and entire, wanting nothing (James 1:4).

Great people give praise; little people seek it.

———◆•◆———

Let another man praise thee, and not thine own mouth
(Proverbs 27:2).

Don't fear tomorrow. God is already there.

---◆•◆---

And God said unto Moses, I AM THAT I AM (Exodus 3:14).

I have never met a man who has given me as much trouble as myself.

(Dwight L. Moody)

———— ◆•◆ ————

But grow in grace, and in the knowledge of our Lord and Saviour Jesus Christ. To him be glory both now and for ever. Amen (2 Peter 3:18).

I know the Bible is inspired because it inspires me.

(Dwight L. Moody)

◆•◆

Thy word is a lamp unto my feet, and a light unto my path
(Psalm 119:105).

Faith with works is a force; faith without works is a farce.

◆•◆

Faith without works is dead (James 2:20).

Everyone must row with the oars he has.

(English proverb)

———◆•◆———

Now there are diversities of gifts, but the same Spirit. And there are differences of administrations, but the same Lord (1 Corinthians 12:4–5).

Two things a man should never be angry at: what he can help, and what he cannot help.

(Thomas Fuller)

❖

He that is slow to anger is better than the mighty; and he that ruleth his spirit than he that taketh a city (Proverbs 16:32).

Many people forget God all day, then ask Him to remember them at night.

We have one Father, even God (John 8:41).

Grace makes you gracious; the Giver makes you give.

(E. Stanley Jones)

———◆•◆———

*And God is able to make all grace abound toward you
(2 Corinthians 9:8).*

139

There may be love without happiness, but there is never happiness without love.

He that keepeth the law, happy is he (Proverbs 29:18).

Today is the first day of the rest of your life.

———◆•◆———

This is the day which the Lord hath made; we will rejoice and be glad in it (Psalm 118:24).

Better to limp all the way to heaven than not get there at all.

———◆•◆———

An inheritance incorruptible, and undefiled, and that fadeth not away, reserved in heaven for you (1 Peter 1:4).

After crosses and losses men grow humbler and wiser.

(Benjamin Franklin)

———◆•◆———

The fear of the Lord is the instruction of wisdom; and before honour is humility (Proverbs 15:33).

If you have no joy in your religion, there's a leak in your Christianity somewhere.

(Billy Sunday)

For his anger endureth but a moment; in his favour is life: weeping may endure for a night, but joy cometh in the morning (Psalm 30:5).

Eternity is now.

◆•◆

The gift of God is eternal life (Romans 6:23).

Whatever a man loves, that is his god

(Martin Luther).

———◆•◆———

Jesus said to him, "You shall love the Lord your God with all your heart, with all your soul, and with all your mind. This is the first and great commandment" (Matthew 22:37-38, NKJV).

Marriages are made in heaven, but they are lived on earth.

(George P. Weiss)

---◆•◆---

But he that is married careth for the things that are of the world, how he may please his wife (1 Corinthians 7:33).

Money never made a man happy yet, nor will it.

(Benjamin Franklin)

The love of money is the root of all evil (1 Timothy 6:10).

No man is poor who has had a godly mother.

(Abraham Lincoln)

—◆•◆—

My son, hear the instruction of thy father, and forsake not the law of thy mother (Proverbs 1:8).

Beware in your prayer, above everything, of limiting God, not only by unbelief, but by fancying that you know what He should do.

(Andrew Murray)

━━━◆•◆━━━

Now unto him that is able to do exceeding abundantly above all that we ask or think, according to the power that worketh in us (Ephesians 3:20).

Anger is never without a reason, but seldom with a good one.

(Benjamin Franklin)

Let not the sun go down upon your wrath (Ephesians 4:26).

Closer is He than breathing, and nearer than hands and feet.

(Alfred, Lord Tennyson)

❖

I sought the Lord, and he heard me, and delivered me from all my fears (Psalm 34:4).

If men are so wicked with religion, what would they be without it?

(Benjamin Franklin)

———◆•◆———

Pure religion and undefiled before God and the Father is this, To visit the fatherless and widows in their affliction, and to keep himself unspotted from the world (James 1:27).

No man knows how bad he is until he has tried to be good.

(C.S. Lewis)

———◆•◆———

There is none that doeth good, no, not one (Romans 3:12).

If your riches are yours, why don't you take them with you t'other world?

(Benjamin Franklin)

◆ • ◆

A good name is rather to be chosen than great riches, and loving favour rather than silver and gold (Proverbs 22:1).

All unbelief is the belief of a lie.

(Horatius Bonar)

Lord, I believe; help thou mine unbelief (Mark 9:24).

Salvation is free, but it is not cheap.

For God so loved the world, that he gave his only begotten Son (John 3:16).

When you point a finger at someone else, remember that three fingers are pointing back at you.

---◆・◆---

First cast out the beam out of thine own eye (Matthew 7:5).

Never, never, never, never give up.

Therefore put on the full armor of God, so that when the day of evil comes, you may be able to stand your ground, and after you have done everything, to stand (Ephesians 6:13, NIV).

The great thing in this world is not so much where we are, but in what direction we are moving.

(Oliver Wendell Holmes)

◆ ● ◆

Brethren, I do not count myself to have apprehended; but one thing I do, forgetting those things which are behind and reaching forward to those things which are ahead, I press toward the goal for the prize of the upward call of God in Christ Jesus (Philippians 3:13–14, NKJV).